Nothing Loopy about This

What Are Loops and Conditionals?

by Brian P. Cleary

illustrations by Martin Goneau

M Millbrook Press • Minneapolis

Coding means giving computers and apps and websites a set of commands

When book opens

SAY Greetings, reader!

End

When book closes

that tells them exactly what each one should do using **language** that it understands.

A **loop** is a part of those coded instructions,
and its job is to always repeat

a portion of **code** a set number of times and then stop when the task is complete.

Loops can save coders a great deal of time
on work that could go on forever,
like giving the same command
eight million times.

So maybe instead of programming a robot to top just one cupcake with frosting,

a **LOOP** could repeat thirty
times and you'd have thirty
done, but it's much
less exhausting!

A **loop** in the code tells a feeder to fill this dish here at eight, NOON, and six

each day all year through—
just by telling it once.
Loops are one of a coder's main tricks!

A whole set of rules that is put into action **if** something occurs has a name:

it's called a **conditional**—and
it's pretty cool—

it plays an **"if . . . then"**
kind of game.

Like, "**If** the temperature's higher than 15, **then** recess will be outside, teachers!

But **if** it is 15 or lower, **then** recess
will be in the gym,
near the bleachers."

Conditionals help when you're writing a code. You'll use **if** and **then** to make rules,

like telling the self-driving car
you're designing
to lower its speed around schools.

The **code** might say **if** it's between
certain hours
and a school is within 90 feet,

then the car will slow down—and will come to a stop

if someone is crossing the street.

Loops and **conditionals** lend a big hand
to code-writing pros of all ages,

like YOU to write software, create fun, new games,

or make your own apps or web pages!

So what are loops and conditionals?

Do you know?

Coding is fun! And best of all, anyone can do it! All you need is a computer or tablet, an internet connection, and a willingness to try.

As you read in this book, loops are sets of instructions that repeat a certain number of times. They're useful in programming repetitive tasks, such as instructing a car to go around a racetrack multiple times. Conditionals let programs respond to different circumstances by telling them to do one thing if a situation is true and another if it is false.

Loops and conditionals make it easier to do things like:

- shelve library books
- build cars in a factory
- listen to a song again
- play a video game
- know when your car needs gas
- take an online personality test

Loops and conditionals save you time and make mistakes less likely. Coding languages that use block coding, such as Scratch and Alice, help make things even easier, because you can drag and drop "blocks" of code to write your program. It's best to start with something simple. Don't worry if your code isn't perfect from the get-go. The more you practice, the easier it will be!

Check out these great resources!

Books

Liukas, Linda. *Hello, Ruby: Adventures in Coding*. New York: Feiwel and Friends, 2015.
This picture and activity book for new coders introduces the basics of computational thinking, such as breaking big problems into smaller ones, finding patterns, and creating step-by-step plans.

Loya, Allyssa. *Disney Coding Adventures: First Steps for Kid Coders*. Minneapolis: Lerner Publications, 2019.
Friendly Disney characters introduce kid coders to the basic concepts of algorithms, bugs and errors, loops, and conditionals. Hands-on activities throughout the book add to the fun.

Robinson, Fiona. *Ada's Ideas: The Story of Ada Lovelace, the World's First Computer Programmer*. New York: Abrams Books for Young Readers, 2016.
This picture book biography introduces trailblazer Ada Byron Lovelace. She loved math and science, and she created the first computer program—even before electronic computers existed.

Websites and Apps

Code.org
https://code.org
This site has lots of resources for anyone who wants to start coding—including students and their teachers. Check out the "Projects" tab to see what other kids have done and take a look at the code for these projects.

Scratch Jr.
https://www.scratchjr.org
This simple, block-based programming language was created especially for early elementary students who don't have any previous coding experience. It runs on both iPads and Android tablets.

Find activities, games, and more at www.brianpcleary.com

ABOUT THE AUTHOR & THE ILLUSTRATOR

BRIAN P. CLEARY is the author of the best-selling Words Are CATegorical® series, as well as the Sounds Like Reading® series, the Poetry Adventures series, and several others. He is also the author of *Crunch and Crack, Oink and Whack! An Onomatopoeia Story* and *The Sun Played Hide-and-Seek: A Personification Story.* He lives in Cleveland, Ohio.

MARTIN GONEAU is the illustrator of many books, including quite a number in the Words Are CATegorical™ series. When he is not drawing, he enjoys playing video games and learning how to code. He lives in Trois-Rivières, Québec, with his lovely wife and his two sons.

Thank you to technical expert Michael Miller for reviewing the text and illustrations.

Text copyright © 2019 by Brian P. Cleary
Illustrations copyright © 2019 by Lerner Publishing Group, Inc.

Millbrook Press
A division of Lerner Publishing Group, Inc.
241 First Avenue North
Minneapolis, MN 55401 USA

For reading levels and more information, look up this title at www.lernerbooks.com.

Main body text set in Chauncy Decaf Medium 27/36. Typeface provided by the Chank Company.
The illustrations in this book were created in Adobe Photoshop using a Wacom Cintiq Pro 16.

Library of Congress Cataloging-in-Publication Data

Names: Cleary, Brian P., 1959- author. | Goneau, Martin, illustrator.
Title: Nothing loopy about this : what are loops and conditionals? / Brian P. Cleary ; illlustrated by Martin Goneau.
Description: Minneapolis : Millbrook Press, [2019] | Series: Coding Is CATegorical | Audience: Age 5-9. | Audience: K to Grade 3. | Includes bibliographical references and index.
Identifiers: LCCN 2018022634 (print) | LCCN 2018028098 (ebook) | ISBN 9781541543867 (eb pdf) | ISBN 9781541533073 (lb : alk. paper) | ISBN 9781541545588 (pb : alk. paper)
Subjects: LCSH: Loop tiling (Computer science)—Juvenile literature. | Conditionals (Logic)—Juvenile literature. | Computer programming—Juvenile literature.
Classification: LCC QA76.6115 (ebook) | LCC QA76.6115 .C44 2019 (print) | DDC 005.4/53—dc23

LC record available at https://lccn.loc.gov/2018022634

Manufactured in the United States of America
1-44876-35726-10/9/2018